NEW SOUTH WALES

NEW SOUTH WALES
THE PREMIER STATE
NH
NEW HOLLAND

INTRODUCTION

New South Wales (NSW) is a south-eastern Australian state, distinguished by its coastal cities, national parks, outback mining towns and wine growing area. It borders with Queensland, Victoria and South Australia and contains the Australian Capital Territory within it.

There is so much to explore in this state from over 1000 kilometres of coastline: the north coast with its natural beauty from headland to hinterland; the central coast which offers surf, sand and serenity; to the south coast where you will find quiet seaside towns and brilliant beaches. Moving inland is the Blue Mountains, which is a World Heritage Site, with its soaring sandstone ridges in native bushland; to the magical Snowy Mountains in the south. The Outback offers big skies, red dirt and endless adventure. In the countryside you will find small town

charm and passionate producers. The Hunter Valley boasts world-class wines and gourmet getaways. The Murray River is Australia's longest river and, off the coast, Lord Howe Island with its coral reefs, crystal-clear water and island life.

Over eight million people reside in NSW and two thirds of the population live in the greater Sydney area. Sydney, the NSW capital, has the most spectacular harbour in the world, and is home to iconic structures such as the Sydney Opera House, Sydney Harbour Bridge and the newly rebuilt Sydney Fish Market. Sydney boasts a very diverse culture. Alongside interesting architectural buildings featured in the city are rooftop bars, theatres and arts entertainment with world-class restaurants. Sydney is classified as one of the world's top tourist destinations.

NORTH COAST

State Border Marker between Queensland and New South Wales Tweed Heads.

Walking track along the Lennox Point Headland in Ballina.

Brunswick Heads.

Fingal Heads looking at Cook Island on the Tweed Coast.

Fingal Head Beach near Tweed Heads in northern New South Wales.

Captain Cook Memorial and Light is located on Point Danger.

Ballina.

Burns Point, Ballina.

Byron Bay.

Cape Byron Lighthouse, Byron Bay.

Byron Bay.

Bryon Bay.

Panoramic view of Byron Bay.

Lismore.

Lismore town centre.

Nimbin.

Nimbin Main Street.

Nimbin.

War Memorial in the town centre of Casino.

Bald Rock is the largest monolith in southern hemisphere situated in Tenterfield.

Panorama of the landscape of Tenterfield.

Tenterfield Post Office.

Disused railway bridge at Tenterfield Creek.

Glen Innes Town Hall.

Stonehenge Recreation Reserve in Glen Innes.

Rangers Valley Cattle Station out near Glen Innes.

Beardy Waters at Glen Innes.

Historic Border Bridge (MacIntyre Bridge) crossing into Goondiwindi QLD from NSW.

Lightning Ridge.

Cattle grid across the road to Lightning Ridge.

Historic Cooper's Cottage, Lightning Ridge.

Lightning Ridge.

Bank Art Museum Moree (BAMM)

The Big Plane at the Amaroo Tavern in Moree.

Inverell Post Office.

Inverell Town Hall.

Grain silos, Inverell.

Yamba.

Yamba Beach and Yamba Ocean Pool.

Yamba Lighthouse, also known as Yamba Light or Clarence Head Light, is an active lighthouse in Wooli Park.

Ten Miles Beach, Bundjalung National Park.

Jetty at Yamba.

Clarence River, Grafton.

Grafton.

Corcoran Park Jetty, Grafton.

Armidale.

Dangars Falls, Armidale.

Dorrigo National Park.

The Wonga Walk in the rainforest of Dorrigo National Park.

Suspension walking bridge, Dorrigo National Park.

Dangar Falls.

Dorrigo.

Brooms Head.

Coastal Red Rock at Brooms Head.

Emerald Beach.

Coffs Harbour.

Coffs Harbour.

Coffs Harbour Jetty.

Big Banana Coffs Harbour.

Diggers Beach at Coffs Harbour.

Coffs Harbour Marina.

Bellinger River, Mylestom.

Sawtell Memorial Rock Pool, Sawtell.

Nambucca River near the entrance to Pacific Ocean at Nambucca Heads.

South West Rocks.

Horseshoe Bay at South West Rocks.

Back Creek Footbridge, South West Rocks.

Trial Bay Gaol, South West Rocks.

Kangaroos playing at South West Rocks.

Crescent Head.

Crescent Head.

Port Macquarie.

Popular tourist spot with cruises around Port Macquarie.

Port Macquarie.

Hastings River near Port Macquarie.

Koala.

Tacking Point Lighthouse at Port Macquarie.

The southern breakwall of Port Macquarie's Hastings River.

Dunbogan Beach to Diamond Head in Crowdy Bay National Park.

Harrington Break Wall and Manning River, Harrington.

Harrington.

Harrington Break Wall and town.

Farquhar Park, Old Bar.

Diamond Head Beach.

The Head Street Bridge across Coolongolook River between the towns of Forster and Tuncurry.

Tuncurry Rock Pool, Forster-Tuncurry estuary.

Wallis Lake between Forster and Tuncurry.

Forster.

Blueys Beach.

Bennetts Beach, also known as Hawks Nest Beach.

Dark Point sand dunes at Myall Lakes National Park.

Nelson Bay Marina.

Dolphin and whale watching charter tour boat in Nelson Bay.

Shoal Bay in the background of Tomaree Mountain and Zenith Beach.

Zenith Beach and Tomaree Headland, Port Stephens.

Nelson Head Lighthouse, Nelson Bay.

Jimmys Beach, Port Stephens Bay.

Soldier's Point.

Anna Bay.

Newcastle.

Nobbys Head Lighthouse on Newcastle Harbour.

Newcastle.

Fort Scratchley, Newcastle.

Downtown Newcastle.

Town Hall building in Newcastle.

Downtown Newcastle.

Newcastle.

Pokolbin, Hunter Valley.

Hunter Valley.

Tyrrell's Wines in the Hunter Valley.

Eastern Grey Kangaroos in the Hunter Valley.

Hunter Valley Gardens, Pokolbin.

Hunter Valley Gardens.

Big Wine Bottle in the Hunter Valley Gardens.

Vineyards in the Hunter Valley.

Hunter Valley.

Hope Estate Vineyard, Hunter Valley.

V FIRM
4 6800
swfirm.com.au
FINANCIAL
PETERS
petersrealestate.com.au
933 7855
40
Fancy Plants
25

Maitland.

Caves Beach.

Swansea at Lake Macquarie.

Swansea Rising Sun Memorial.

Terrigal Boardwalk, Terrigal.

Terrigal.

Terrigal Esplanade, Terrigal.

The Entrance, Central Coast.

Central Coast.

Kilcare, Central Coast.

Avoca Beach.

Gosford.

Point Frederick, Gosford.

Pearl Beach.

Pearl Beach overlooking Lion Island.

Bouddi National Park between Patonga and Pearl Beach.

The Boathouse Hotel, Patonga Beach.

Ettalong Beach.

Australian Reptile Park, Somersby, Central Coast.

Wollomombi Falls, Waterfall Way

INLAND

THUNDERBOLTS WAY CAFE
FRIED CHICKEN
THUNDERBOLTS WAY CAFE
Fenwicke House

Walcha.

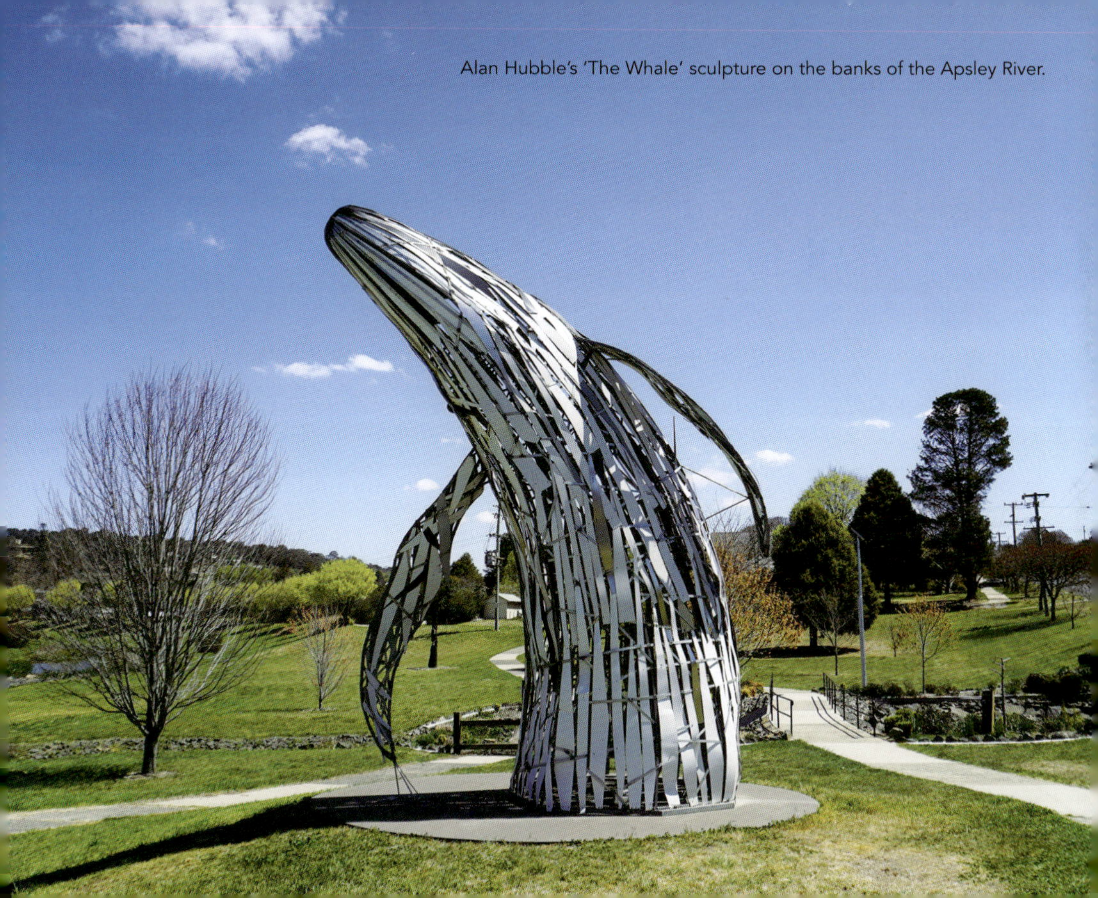

Alan Hubble's 'The Whale' sculpture on the banks of the Apsley River.

Historical Hotel in Walcha.

Tamworth.

DECO
RESTAURANT
CH

CENTRAL HOTEL
regionalaustraliabank
regionalaustraliabank
CH BOUTIQUE HOTEL
Port Macquarie
Armidale
Brisbane
Manilla
BRISBANE ST

Tamworth.

The Big Golden Guitar, Tamworth.

Tamworth.

Gunnedah.

Gunnedah.

Gunnedah.

Gunnedah River.

Gunnedah Miners Memorial.

Grain silos, Gilgandra.

Nyngan.

Entering the town of Cobar.

Fort Bourke Hill Lookout, Cobar.

St Laurence O'Toole Catholic Church, Cobar.

Cobar Station.

Darling River around Wilcannia on the Barrier Highway.

White Cliffs, an opal town.

White Cliffs opal fields.

Mungo National Park.

The Living Desert and Sculptures, Broken Hill.

The Sculptures Walk.

Mundi Mundi lookout sign near Silverton and Broken Hill.

Entry into Silverton.

Mad Max 2 Museum, Silverton.

SILVE
AVAILABLE HERE!
NOTICE
17
16

Silverton Hotel, Silverton.

An outback road to Broken Hill.

Broken Hill.

Broken Hill.

Broken Hill Post Office.

Homestead in Broken Hill.

Theatre Royal Hotel, Broken Hill.

Broken Hill.

Broken Hill city lookout.

Broken HIll.

The Big Bench, Broken Hill.

A mine building in Broken Hill.

Ivanhoe Station.

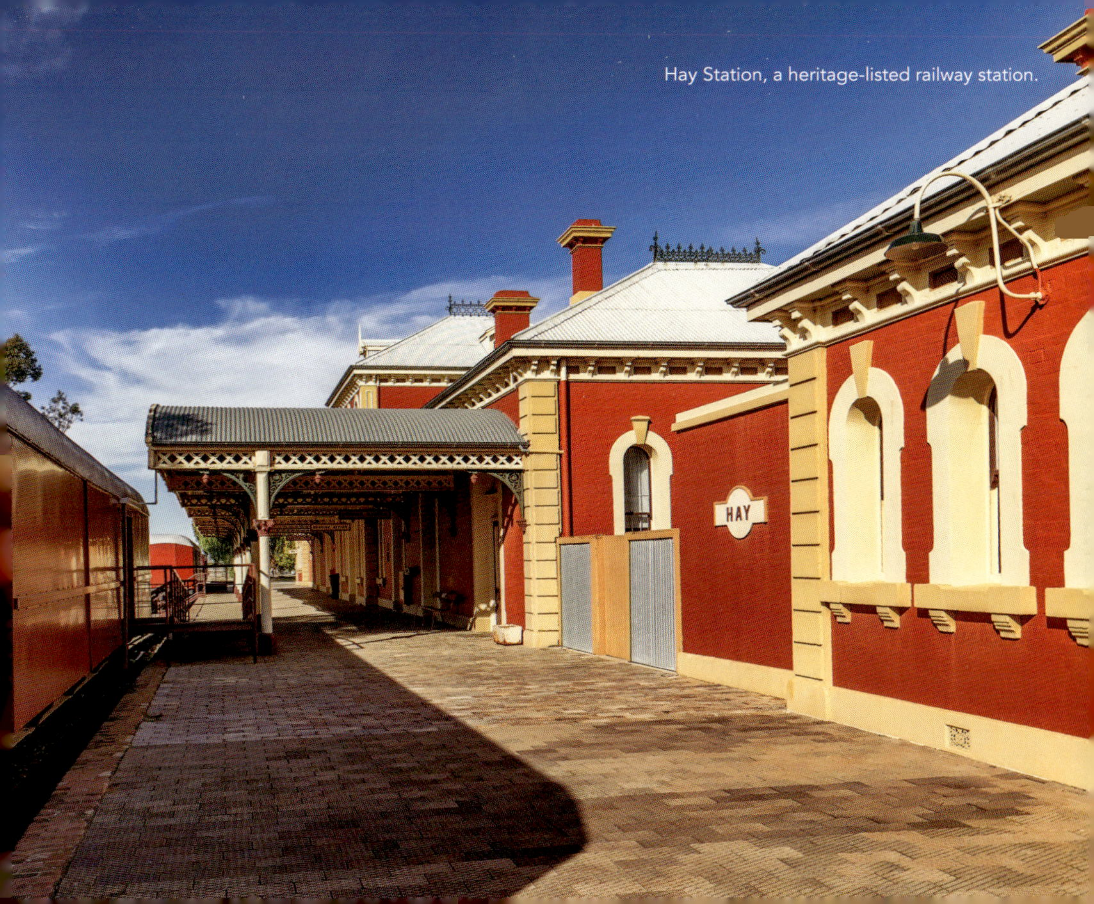

Hay Station, a heritage-listed railway station.

Deniliquin in the Riverina.

'Cut' sculpture by Jonathan Leahy, Deniliquin.

Home in Deniliqin.

Albury.

Albury.

Albury.

Albury Railway Station.

The Ettamogah Pub near Albury.

The Harold Mair Bridge, Albury.

St Matthew's Church, Albury.

Murrumbidgee River
in Wagga Wagga.

Wagga Wagga Station.

Wagga Wagga.

Wagga Wagga.

Fairey Firefly Memorial, Griffith.

Griffith City Council building.

Farmland in Cowra.

Cowra.

Forbes Town Hall.

Forbes Post Office.

Victoria Park with the Court House in Forbes.

Murriyang, CSIRO Parkes Radio Telescope, a.k.a. 'The Dish'

Parkes, where the Elvis festival is held every year.

Mudgee, wine growing region.

Lake Windamere on the Cudgegong River, south of Mudgee.

Mudgee Memorial Clock commemorating the 50th Anniversary of World War II, near St Mary of the Presentation Catholic Church.

Mudgee.

Gulgong Pioneers Museum.

Dubbo.

Dubbo Rail Bridge over Macquarie River.

Dubbo.

Old Dubbo Gaol in Dubbo.

Dubbo War Memorial.

Rhinoceros at Taronga Western Plains Zoo, Dubbo.

Wellington Caves, 8 km south of Wellington.

ACCOMMODATION
The

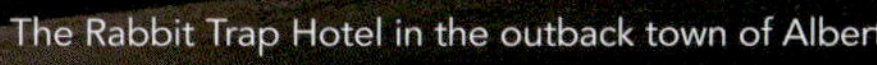

The Rabbit Trap Hotel in the outback town of Albert.

Town of Orange.

Orange town centre.

Farmland in Orange.

Orange.

Bathurst.

Bathurst War Memorial and Bathurst War Memorial Carillon.

Pit Straight Mount Panorama, Bathurst.

Mount Panorama Motor Racing Circuit, Bathurst.

Lithgow.

Hassans Walls Lookout near Lithgow.

Lithgow Blast Furnace.

Hassans Walls near Lithgow.

Jenolan River Walking Track.

River Cave in Jenolan Caves, Blue Mountains.

The Three Sisters, Blue Mountains.

Lizard in the Blue Mountains.

Grand Canyon Walking Track, Blue Mountains National Park.

Wentworth Falls in the Blue Mountains.

Scenic Skyway, a cable-car crossing the Jamison Valley, Blue Mountains National Park.

Echo Point lookout, Katoomba, Blue Mountains.

Sydney Harbour Bridge.

Sydney Opera House, Sydney.

Sydney Harbour.

Cockatoo Island.

Old prison on Cockatoo Island.

Art Gallery of New South Wales.

Hyde Park Barracks Museum.

Museum of Contemporary Art Australia in the Rocks, Sydney.

The James Craig vessel from the Sydney Heritage Fleet in Pyrmont.

Taronga Zoo Sydney.

Parramatta, Sydney.

Manly Beach, Manly.

Long Reef.

Mona Vale Beach.

Mona Vale Beach.

Whale Beach, Sydney.

Palm Beach, Sydney.

Bondi Icebergs Pool.

Bondi Beach.

LIFEGUARD

One of the world's most famous beaches, Bondi Beach.

Port Botany, Sydney.

Bare Island Fort, Kamay Botany
Bay National Park, La Perouse

Little Bay, Sydney.

Congwong Beach, La Perouse.

Cronulla Beach.

SOUTH COAST

Port Kembla, Wollongong.

Kiama.

Berry.

Hampden Bridge, a historic suspension bridge across the Kangaroo River.

Fitzroy Falls near Bowral.

Bowral.

Shoalhaven River Bridge, Nowra.

Jervis Bay.

Cunjurong Point inlet,
Lake Conjola.

Mollymook Beach.

Merimbula.

Eden.

Olympia Cinema Theatre, Bombala.

Goulburn Post Office.

The Big Merino, nicknamed 'Rambo', in Goulburn.

Cooma.

Clarke Gorge of Snowy Mountains National Park.

Jindabyne Lake in the Snowy Mountains.

Lake Crackenback in Thredbo Valley of Kosciuszko National Park.

Perisher Valley.

Snowy Mountains National Park.

Australian Snowy mountains from top of Mount Perisher overlooking Perisher Valley.

First published in 2025 by New Holland Publishers

newhollandpublishers.com

A record of this book is held at the National Library of Australia.

ISBN 9781760798451

Managing Director: Fiona Schultz
General Manager: Olga Dementiev
Designer: Andrew Davies
Production Director: Arlene Gippert

Keep up with New Holland Publishers:

NewHollandPublishers

@newhollandpublishers